DAVID CROCKETT

CREATING A LEGEND

MARY DODSON WADE

ILLUSTRATIONS BY

JOY FISHER HEIN

1786-1836

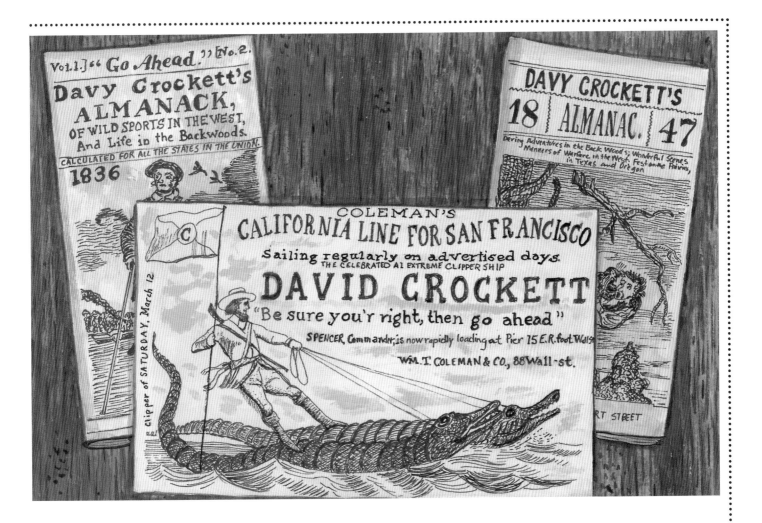

DAVID AND "DAVY"

David Crockett told tall tales about himself. They made people laugh. People loved these made-up stories. They made up more. They said "Davy" could hug a bear. They said "Davy" rode alligators. The stories were not real.

David Crockett was a real person. He did many interesting things. When he died at the Alamo, he became a **legend**.

David was born in Tennessee (ten-ih-SEE) in 1786. His family was very poor.

David's father built a **tavern**. Wagon drivers stopped there. When David was twelve, his father hired him to help a wagon driver. David walked through deep snow to get home.

The next year he went to school for four days. He got into a fight with a bully and played hooky. His father got angry. David ran away from home.

Three years later David came back. His father owed money. David worked a whole year to pay his father's **debts**.

The man he worked for taught him to read. David learned to write his name. He put two big loops under it.

MARRYING A WIFE

David was twenty when he married Polly Finley. They had a farm. Before long, they had two boys. Then David went off to fight Creek Indians.

After he returned home, his little girl was born. But his wife died. David needed help to care for his children.

Elizabeth Patton lived nearby. She was a **widow** with two children. David knew she was a good mother. At their wedding he chased her squealing pet pig out of the house.

BEAR HUNTER

David moved his family to middle Tennessee. He had bad luck in business. A flood washed away his mills for grinding corn and making gunpowder. A boat sank with all the things he had to sell.

He moved west again. David and Elizabeth had three more children by then. He fed his family and others by hunting bears. He never missed when he shot his rifle.

Friends chose him to make laws for Tennessee. When he was forty-one, he became **Congressman** from Tennessee.

Everyone in Washington knew him. Someone wrote a play. The main **character** was named Nimrod Wildfire. Nimrod carried a rifle and wore an animal skin cap. People knew Nimrod was pretending to be David.

David went to see the play. The actor came over and bowed to him. David bowed back.

Then someone wrote a book about him. Many things in it were not true. David's friend helped him write his own story.

PICTURES

While he was in Washington, David had his picture painted. His dark hair was slicked down. He said, "I look like a cross between a **Congressman** and a Methodist (METH-uh-dist) preacher!"

David asked the artist to paint him as a hunter. He got a rifle, hunting clothes, and an old **felt** hat. He found stray dogs. The artist wanted to use his own dog, but David didn't like the dog's tail.

After six years, someone else took David's place as Tennessee **Congressman**. He was fifty years old. Everything he had tried seemed to fail. He took his rifle and started to Texas.

On the way he ran out of money. A man gave him $30 for his watch.

When David got to Texas, he wrote his family a letter. "This is the garden spot of the world."

AT THE ALAMO

David went to San Antonio (san an-TOE-nee-o). He wanted to help free Texas from Mexico. Soon, three thousand Mexican soldiers marched into the city. David and others raced inside an old **mission** called the Alamo.

Mexican General Santa Anna put up a red flag. People in the Alamo would die if they did not give up. The men would not give up.

On March 6, 1836, Mexican soldiers came over the wall. David and all the other men in the Alamo were killed.

IT HAPPENED LATER

Six weeks after David died, Texans won the battle at San Jacinto (san jah-SIHN-toe). Texas was free.

The man who had David's watch sent it back to Elizabeth. Later she moved to Texas. She lived on land given to men who had fought for Texas.

People made up wild stories about "Davy" Crockett. The real David Crockett was a great hunter and storyteller. He was never rich, but he was a real hero.

GLOSSARY

character—a person in a story or play

Congressman—a member of Congress who makes laws

debts—money that a person owes

felt—wool pressed flat into thick cloth

legend—a famous person everyone knows about

mission—a place built by churches to teach people

tavern—a place to eat and sleep

DAVID CROCKETT'S LIFE

1786, August 17—born in east Tennessee

1806—married Polly Finley

1813–1814—soldier in Creek Indian war

1815—married Elizabeth Patton

1821—elected to make Tennessee laws

1827—Congressman from Tennessee

1836, January—came to Texas

1836, March 6—died at the Alamo in San Antonio, Texas

MORE TO KNOW

BOOKS:

Adler. David A. *A Picture Book of Davy Crockett.* New York: Holiday House, 1998.
Alphin, Elaine Marie. *Davy Crockett.* Minneapolis MN: Lerner Publishing, 2002.
Krensky, Stephen. *Davy Crockett: A Life on the Frontier.* New York: Aladdin, 2004.

WEBSITES:

"David 'Davy' Crockett (1786-1836),"
http://www.lsjunction.com/people/crockett.htm
[This website site has a picture of David Crockett.]

"Davy Crockett: A Folktale for Reading Out Loud,"
http://www.activated-storytellers.com/folktales/davy_crockett.html
[Tall tales adapted from some those David Crockett told. Real information given as well.]

PLACES TO VISIT:

Replicas of cabins and tavern where David Crockett lived:
Davy Crockett Birthplace State Park, Limestone TN
Davy Crockett Cabin/Museum, Rutherford TN.
http://www.davycrockettcabin.org/
Davy Crockett Tavern, Morristown, TN

MARY DODSON WADE, a former educator and librarian, is the author of more than fifty books for children, including *Christopher Columbus, Cinco de Mayo, I Am Houston, I'm Going to Texas/Yo Voy a Tejas, President's Day, C.S. Lewis: The Chronicler of Narnia* and *Joan Lowery Nixon: Masterful Mystery Writer.* She and her husband live in Houston, Texas, and enjoy traveling.

JOY FISHER HEIN is an artist, a gardener and the illustrator of the award-winning *Miss Ladybird's Wildflowers.* She has been selected as the artist for the 2009 Texas Reading Club. She was also selected by the City of San Antonio to create thirteen large art panels for Walker Ranch Historic Park. She and her husband, artist Frank Hein, live in the Texas Hill Country, where Joy is a Texas Master Naturalist and is certified to create Schoolyard Habitats for the National Wildlife Federation.

Look for more **Texas Heroes for Young Readers**
from Bright Sky Press: